DESERT

EARTH'S BIOMES

DESERT

TOM WARHOL

Marshall Cavendish
Benchmark
New York

To my brothers and sisters Joan, Dave, Bob, Mike, John, Steve, Jim, and Marianne and the common interest we all share in the natural world.

Marshall Cavendish Benchmark
99 White Plains Road
Tarrytown, New York 10591
www.marshallcavendish.us

Text, maps, and illustrations copyright © 2007 by Marshall Cavendish Corporation
Maps by Robert Romagnoli

Editor: Karen Ang
Editorial Director: Michelle Bisson
Art Director: Anahid Hamparian
Series Designer: Patrice Sheridan

Library of Congress Cataloging-in-Publication Data
Warhol, Tom.
Desert / by Tom Warhol.
p. cm. — (Earth's biomes)
Summary: "Explores desert biomes and covers where they are located as well
as the plants and animals that inhabit them"—Provided by publisher.
Includes bibliographical references and index.
ISBN-13: 978-0-7614-2194-8
ISBN-10: 0-7614-2194-7
1. Deserts—Juvenile literature. 2. Desert ecology—Juvenile literature.
I. Title. II. Series.

QH88.W37 2007
577.54—dc22

2006015823

Front cover caption: A sand dune
Title page: A desert landscape
Back cover: Salt flats

Photo research by Candlepants, Inc.
The photographs in this book are used by permission and through the courtesy of:
Minden Pictures: Yva Momatiuk/John Eastcott, 2, 24; Tim Fitzharris, 11 ; Mitsuaki Iwago, 23; Frans Lanting, 26, 34; Carr Clifton, 29, 73; Shin Yoshino, 31; Michael & Patricia Fogden, 32, 48, 49, 64, 67; Mark Moffett, 35; Cyril Ruoso\JH Editorial, 43; Tom Vezo, 47; Tui De Roy, 50, 68; Will Meinderts/Foto Natura, 52; ZSSD, 59. *Tom Warhol:* 7, 30, 46. *Corbis:* Bob Krist, 8; Paul Almasy, 15; Michele Westmorland, 17; David Muench, 20, back cover; George H. H. Huey, 38; Keren Su, 60; Ludovic Maisant, 62; Charles O'Rear, 69. *Photo Researchers Inc.:* Nigel J. Dennis, 13; Georg Gerster, 19; Paul Stepan, 37; Art Wolfe, 42; Jeff Lepore, 45; Steve Cooper, 54; George Holton, 61; .Nigel J. Dennis, 66; Ray Ellis, 71; US Department of Energy, 72. *Peter Arnold:* Michael Bader, 57.

Printed in China

1 3 5 6 4 2

CONTENTS

Introduction A Dry and Peaceful Land   6

1   What Makes a Desert?   9

2   Landforms   17

3   Adaptations   27

4   Hot Deserts   39

5   Temperate Deserts   51

6   Coastal Deserts   63

Conclusion So Harsh, Yet So Delicate   70

Glossary   74

Find Out More   76

Bibliography   77

Index   79

INTRODUCTION

A DRY AND PEACEFUL LAND

The hot sun beats down upon the sand, making the surface too hot to touch. Not a thing moves. It is as though the whole landscape is waiting for this hottest part of the day to end.

Winds scatter sand off the dunes and across the dry riverbed, startling a coyote resting in the shade of a cholla cactus. The canine bolts upright, catching the tip of a cholla branch on its fur, and trots swiftly to the other side of the riverbed with the cholla tip lodged in its fur. There it will take shelter behind a larger mesquite tree. As it settles under the tree, the coyote knocks a few fence lizards from their branches. They were perched there, above the hot ground, being cooled by the wind. The lizards scramble back into the shade of the tree as soon as they hit the sand. The coyote scratches the piece of cholla out of its fur. In the cooler and moister soil beneath the mesquite tree, this cholla tip will sprout roots. It will eventually grow into a large plant the size of its parent.

Clouds roll in with the wind, darkening the sky. The open, sparse desert echoes with the sound of loud thunderclaps. The desert seems to hold its breath, as though waiting out the infrequent summer storm that now rains down from the gray clouds. Water falls straight and heavy, drenching the sand, and rolling quickly off any high points of land. The dry riverbed receives this water, swelling into a raging river in a matter of minutes. The coyote quickly jumps up once again, avoiding this powerful flood.

Just downstream, where the riverbed squeezes between sandstone cliffs, the water surge is intense, carrying away the loose soil along the banks. As the cliffs fall away and the sands level out farther downstream, the floodwater spreads out, diffusing its power and leaving tons of sediment behind.

Some water seeps down into the soil, but much of it evaporates quickly as the sun breaks through the clouds, heating the sands to unbearable temperatures again. The coyote is on the hunt, taking advantage of the small rodents that were displaced, like him, by the sudden floods. After a successful chase and a tasty meal, he finds a small, rocky overhang on the shady side of a low hill and settles in. He waits for the pounding sun to be once again obscured by clouds or for night to offer a break from the heat.

One of the most clever and adaptable mammals in the United States, the coyote can be found in almost any habitat in the country, but it is perhaps most common in southwestern deserts.

Although deserts are far from being lifeless places, vegetation can grow very sparsely there, like this stunted conifer on a hillside in the California desert.

1

WHAT MAKES A DESERT?

The first impression most people have of deserts is a lifeless, sandy landscape that stretches for miles. However, this is only true of one type of desert landscape. In reality there are a variety of different habitats that make up the desert biome.

Some deserts are relatively rich in species of plants and animals. In many cases, the life-forms that do exist in deserts are unique to this biome. They would have to be, since the environmental conditions—dry climate, winds, sandy soils, salt flats—force anything that lives here to be very resilient and resourceful.

Deserts are one of the most widespread of all biomes. They cover more than 30 percent of Earth's surface, and they occur from the Arctic plains to the equator. Most of the continent of Australia is desert. Not only do deserts cover a lot of land, but they are also constantly changing in size. As the climate changes over long periods of time—more or less rain and wind, higher or lower temperatures—the extent of the deserts shrinks and expands.

Deserts can be divided into two broad categories—hot deserts and temperate deserts. All of the world's hot deserts lie between 20 degrees and 30 degrees North and South latitude, also known as the horse latitudes. Temperate deserts are usually found deep in the interior of large continents, far from any major water source.

Some of the landforms that make up the deserts of the world, especially the hot deserts, are vast, flat plains of pale-colored soils, sand fields, dunes, and mountains, usually cut into by dry riverbeds. However, the main factors that determine where deserts form are global weather patterns, location, and, of course, the availability of water.

HIGH-PRESSURE SYSTEMS

Deserts lie where they do on Earth because of a very regular pattern of planetary air movement. Air rises and falls in six major air cells—three each in the Northern and Southern Hemispheres. The cell that causes dry weather in most of the world's deserts is called the tropical or Hadley cell.

The hottest part of the planet is along the equator. As the Earth rotates on its axis and around its orbit, the equatorial line is always the part of the Earth that is closest to the Sun. As the air along the equator is heated by the Sun it rises into the atmosphere, drawing moisture up with it. This moisture is released as rain when the air mass reaches a certain level, cools, and is drawn toward either the North or South Pole (depending upon which side of the equator the air mass is on). This moisture helps to create the rain forests found near the equator.

With most of its moisture gone, the cold air mass begins to sink toward Earth. The air heats up and dries out as it falls. This hot, dry air, called a high-pressure cell, keeps moisture from forming where the air settles. These regions are where most of the world's hot deserts lie.

High temperatures in the summer make life difficult in the desert. Because there is so little moisture in these regions, there is also very little cloud cover. Like a blanket, clouds help to hold in heat absorbed

Hot deserts, like the Sonoran Desert in North America, attain some of the highest temperatures during the day. Nighttime temperatures drop sharply because of the few clouds, sparse vegetation, and reflective soil color.

from the sun. Without this cloud cover, much of the warmth that desert soils and rocks absorb during the day is quickly lost at night, resulting in cold temperatures. There can be as much as a 36-degree-Fahrenheit (20-degree-Celsius) difference between day and nighttime temperatures in hot deserts.

LOCATION

The farther a land area is from the ocean or other large body of water, the more likely it is that the land will be very dry. Depending upon terrain, weather, and other factors, different habitats may form, usually grassland, sparse woodland, or desert.

The expanses of desert throughout Central Asia are far from any oceans. This includes the driest desert outside of the high-pressure zones, the Taklamakan Desert in western China. Other examples include the Great Basin Desert in the United States and the deserts of Iran. These temperate deserts have very cold winters and very hot summers. Frost may even form on some winter nights.

However, deserts do not have to be far from water. A large mountain range may trap moist ocean air and rain passing over it, causing the land on the far side of the mountains to be dry. This "rain-shadow" effect often occurs on the western coasts of continents or islands, fairly close to water.

As air blowing in from the oceans rises up the mountain slopes, it begins to cool, forms clouds, and loses its moisture as rain on the ocean—or windward—side of the mountain. By the time the air reaches the very high peaks and begins to descend the opposite, leeward side of the mountain, the air heats up and actually pulls moisture away from the land. This occurs in many regions of the world, including the Patagonian desert in South America. There, the long Andes Mountain chain prevents Pacific Ocean moisture from reaching much of the interior of the continent.

Another way that deserts are formed is the hardest to understand, and it creates some of the Earth's driest desert formations. Among the many regularly occurring winds on the planet are those that form over the oceans. Winds blowing northward along the west coasts of continents, such as in South America and western Africa, carry away moisture from onshore breezes. These winds also move the warm surface waters with them, which causes colder water to rise from the ocean depths. Very little rain falls on these coastal deserts, such as the Atacama in Chile and the Namib in Namibia, but they are not without moisture. Because of the difference in temperatures between the cold ocean and the warmer air, fog forms along the coasts in the summer. This not only provides vital moisture to the plants and animals living there, but it also helps to keep air temperatures mild.

SPARSE RAINFALL

Most deserts receive less than 24 inches (600 mm) of rain in a year. But less than 1 inch (25 mm) of rain falls each year in the driest deserts. This isn't much for plants or animals to work with. As a result, the driest deserts support the lowest number of life-forms.

Rain may fall in a particular season in deserts, or it may fall sporadically and unpredictably. In temperate deserts, rains tend to occur more often in winter. However, sometimes seasons or even years may pass without a drop of rain.

At other times, one large storm may bring the whole year's rainfall in just a few hours. So much water falls so quickly that the ground cannot absorb it. The surface particles become saturated, creating a barrier

Desert flowers quickly take advantage of any moisture that comes their way. This Kalahari soapbush in South Africa's Kalahari Desert is flowering abundantly after a rainstorm.

to further water penetration. Rainwater runs quickly downhill and, depending upon the terrain, will funnel into canyon streams or spread over a wide, flat area.

Normally only receiving a maximum of 2 inches of rain annually, the Mojave Desert in North America absorbed over 6 inches in the winter of 2004–2005. This was the wettest year on record for the Mojave. The desert was able to hold on to much of this water because the rain fell as light drizzle over a long period, which is an unusual occurrence. Tourists flocked from all across the United States to see the amazing abundance of wildflowers that were able to germinate and flower because of the moisture.

WATER IN THE DESERT

It may seem odd that the most important element for deserts is in such short supply. Most rain that falls on deserts either flows away from arid, or dry, regions or flows underground, out of reach of most plants and animals.

Many large rivers start in mountainous regions and flow through the deserts, bringing much-needed moisture and more fertile soils to the parched landscape. The Nile River in Africa, the Murray-Darling River in Australia, and the Colorado River in North America are examples. These rivers usually empty into an ocean.

Some rivers are like ghosts, briefly appearing and then disappearing. These intermittent rivers and streams are caused by infrequent heavy rains. Water flows quickly overland, channeled into normally dry stream- and riverbeds. These are called *wadis* on the Arabian Peninsula, *oueds* in the Middle East, and *arroyos* in the deserts of North and South America. When heavier than usual rains fall, these riverbeds become channels for rainwater, which scours the beds and edges with its force. If the flood is severe, huge loads of soil will be carried along, and most

Most human settlement in the deserts of Africa lie along river banks. Here, the Nile River flows through the Nubian Desert, the eastern part of the Sahara Desert, in Sudan.

plants may be pulled out and washed away. Residents of desert areas know to stay away from these dry riverbeds if there is any chance of a storm.

More unusual are those rivers that begin within desert regions. These are usually fed by groundwater, which collects in underground caverns and between rock layers. Water in some of these aquifers, as they are called, may be thousands of years old. Desert river water often collects in depressions and evaporates before reaching an outlet such as the sea.

In places where water pools for longer periods of time, along rivers or above aquifers, plants may grow more thickly and help to form an oasis. These fertile spots provide water and cover for many animals. If the water is reliable enough, human settlement and even farming may be possible.

Some plants, especially shrubs, actually channel water down into the soil along their stems and roots. This underground supply will be helpful to the plant during dry periods. Holes burrowed into the soil by earthworms, termites, and beetles also funnel water underground, away from the evaporative action of the Sun.

15

The bright reddish colors of these sand dunes in the Namib Desert are caused by iron oxides in the sand. As the dunes age, more iron is oxidized, creating brighter and brighter colors.

2

LANDFORMS

The makeup of the soil, how the landscape or surface terrain is arranged, and the underlying geology all influence how water flows and where it stays in the desert. This in turn governs where plants can grow, where animals can forage, and even where humans can settle.

There are two main types of deserts, based on geology. Shield-platform deserts are made up of rocky plains and lowlands with widely scattered ancient volcanic mountains. The majority of the world's deserts are this type and can be found in Africa, the Arabian Peninsula, Australia, and India.

Basin and range deserts include the Great Basin Desert of North America and the Gobi Desert of China. These are made up of younger mountain ranges separated by valleys filled with alluvium, which is soil brought down from the mountain heights by water.

SEAS OF SAND

Sand fields formed over thousands of years when low-lying areas between mountains served as traps for wind-blown sand. Along with dunes, sand fields make up 20 to 50 percent of the landscape of hot deserts and are most common in the Rub' al-Khali, or Empty Quarter, of Saudi Arabia. Here the sands cover 216,000 square miles (560,000 km²).

Underneath the fluid sands are, usually, very hard rock or compacted soils that do not absorb moisture. When rain falls on the sands, it swiftly percolates down to the base of the dune or field. Plants often grow around these dune edges to take advantage of the moisture as it slowly seeps out.

DUNES

Wind plays an important role in deserts. It moves large amounts of soil around, covering much of the world's deserts with sand. About half of the sand fields of hot deserts exist as sand dunes.

Dunes may actually "move" under the action of wind. Wind blowing around a dune carries sand from the gently sloping side to the steeper, leeward slope. In this way, the dune moves, or rolls, with the wind. Mobile sand dunes are called *ergs* in the Arab world.

The shapes and sizes of dunes change constantly, depending on wind intensity and direction, but they can be grouped into a few simple categories: linear, star, and barkhan dunes. They range in size from tiny dunes that form as wind whips around bushes to sand ridges many miles long that build up on the leeward side of rocky hills. Dunes also form as sand collects in shallow depressions.

Linear dunes are the most common and cover large areas of the Australian deserts and the Namib. They can reach nearly 600 feet (183 meters) high and several miles long and lie parallel to each other, making the landscape look striped. Linear dunes grow in the direction of the prevailing wind but are more stable than other moving or growing dunes. Plants can be found growing thickly along their bases.

Dunes are dynamic features of deserts, constantly changing and forming new shapes, such as this star dune in the Namib Desert of Africa.

Star dunes form in areas where the wind direction varies throughout the year. As winds buffet all sides of a small sand hill, a pyramid shape forms, with arms radiating out from the center. These arms acts as traps for more sand, so that star dunes can grow to very large sizes, as much as 3,300 feet (1,000 m) wide and 990 feet (300 m) high. Algeria's Great Eastern Sand Sea contains huge areas of these dunes.

Barkhan dunes move at much greater speeds than other mobile dunes. A 30-foot-high barkhan dune may move 15 to 30 feet (5 to 10 m) in a year. When dunes move as whole fields, they may gradually envelop farms, villages, and even cities, and there is little that the residents can do to stop them.

SALT FLATS

The Great Salt Lake in the state of Utah and the Kavir Desert in central Iran are examples of salt flats. The heavy concentrations of salt are left over from large lakes or inland seas that evaporated over time. Rain simply can't penetrate these hard crusts, but it will pool on the surface. As the water evaporates due to the merciless sun and hot temperatures, mineral salts continue to build.

In Iran, these salts actually hold water beneath them. There is little reason to go to the Kavir Desert because it is so harsh and lifeless, but

The salt crust of the lake bed of Great Salt Lake in Utah is exposed during droughts. As the water evaporates, a salt crust forms, which cracks as it dries and contracts.

also because it is dangerous. These salt crusts can break, exposing a murky soil soup beneath, where people could drown.

Salines, as salt flats are generally called, are known by different names in the many regions of the world where they occur. *Salina, salar, chott, sebka,* and *playa* are just a few terms used to describe the flats.

ROCKS

In shield-platform deserts, such as the Arabian Desert, the bedrock—huge masses of rock that lie beneath soils and cover most of the Earth's land surface—is exposed in elevated plateaus called *hammadas.*

In desert regions where there are extremes of hot and cold temperatures, rocks may become fractured by freezing water that works its way into cracks. The rocks can shatter as the water expands with freezing, and the fragments litter the ground, adding to the soil layers.

Another rocky landform, desert pavement, is known as *regs* in the Arabian Desert. Although "pavement" may sound man-made, this is a naturally occurring landform made up of gravel and small stones that are flattened and compacted. It is formed as sand and softer bedrock are gradually eroded away. The harder rocks are left behind, forming a tight, weather-resistant surface. Desert pavement makes up about 80 percent of the Sahara and about 40 to 50 percent of other deserts.

Many of these stones are covered with a dark brown or black varnish called desert patina. The patina is formed by minerals like iron and manganese oxides that become dissolved as rainwater seeps into the rock. As the sun heats up the rock, it draws this solution out and evaporates the water, leaving behind the minerals as a crust on the surface. Microscopic bacteria and fungi live beneath this patina, helping to bring the minerals to the surface.

All of these exposed rock surfaces absorb little or no moisture, and plants cannot take root here. Most water runs right off these surfaces and channels into normally dry riverbeds, called *wadis* in Saudi Arabia. The rainwater then becomes absorbed into the soil or continues to flow into larger rivers. Plants can only survive in those few areas where water pools, or along the edges of *wadis,* where soils retain water.

MOUNTAINS AND BUTTES

Most desert mountains look so imposing because they rise very steeply from flat plains. Some are made up of piles of hard igneous rocks, which were formed beneath the Earth's surface. These mountains have a much more varied shape. There are many spaces between rocks for plants to take root and for animals to hide.

Other mountains are made of sedimentary rocks, horizontal layers of compressed soil of different origins and consistencies laid down over millions of years. These range from hard sandstones to softer limestones.

Buttes are hills with flat tops formed from sedimentary rocks. Sedimentary rocks vary in their resistance to erosion. Softer rock layers are worn down more easily by wind and rain. Harder layers take longer to wear down, and many buttes today are capped with these hard layers. Uluru—also known as Ayers Rock—in central Australia is an example of an isolated butte. Uluru has experienced massive geologic change over millennia. Unlike other buttes with horizontal layers, it has been tilted and uplifted so that its compressed sandstone layers are vertical.

Other desert hills look like colorful staircases, with plants growing in collected soil on the various steps and lichen and mosses on the vertical risers. These hills formed from different rates of weathering of the many layers of compressed rock.

Uluru in Australia's Northern Territory is an example of an inselberg, or isolated mountain rising from a plain.

BAJADAS

When water falls on desert mountains, it runs down the steep rock faces with powerful force, cutting deep channels and carrying a lot of sediment and debris with it. As this flood of water and soil emerges from the high ground and spreads out into the valleys, it slows down and deposits its sediment load gradually.

At the point where the streams emerge from the mountain, layers of large rocks and even boulders can be found. The farther away from the mountain, the smaller the sediment becomes, until the smallest particles—the clays—are deposited on the valley floor.

Desert rocks and soil were formed from the layers of soil that settled into large inland seas and became compressed by the weight of the water and the upper layers of soil. The layers can be seen in these rocks in Utah's Grand Staircase-Escalante National Monument. They continue to be shaped today by wind and rain.

These graduated soil beds are called alluvial fans when they issue from a single stream. When many streams emerge from a mountain range, the fans may join together in spreading aprons around the high ground called *bajadas* or piedmont. These layers of deep soil are important sites for plants, as they are richer in nutrients and moisture than most of the surrounding areas.

DESERT SOILS

In all biomes, soils develop in concert with plant and animal life. Dead and decaying leaves, animal skins, and animal bodies are eaten and broken down by a wide variety of bacteria, fungi, and insects. They turn into soil elements like nutrients that plants can use for food. This activity reaches its peak in temperate forests.

Water, as rain, weathers rocks and soils, releasing and making nutrients available to plant life. Since deserts, by their very nature, are dry ecosystems, soils tend to be less weathered and thus less nutrient-rich than moister ecosystem soils. The weathering by rain that does occur carries salts in the surface soil down to lower layers. As the water drains away, the concentrated salts are left behind and can form a hard layer know as a salt pan. Very few plants can grow in these salty soils. As a result, desert plant life is much more sparsely distributed than plant life of temperate forests. Fewer plants mean less dead plant matter falls to the ground.

However, the sparsely scattered plants serve as traps for windblown leaves and seeds. The shade from the plants helps the soil retain moisture, and the dead plant matter on the ground enriches the soil. This plant food attracts fungi, worms, ants, and beetles. These organisms attract other animals, like birds and rodents, which, in turn, attract predators like foxes, coyotes, and hawks.

These African elephants are bathing in and drinking the water that has collected in this waterhole during the rainy season in the Kalahari. Soon the water will evaporate, and the elephants will need to find a new source.

3

ADAPTATIONS

Survival in the desert depends upon finding water and avoiding or enduring the heat. Water is the main factor controlling the type, number, and location of plants that grow in the desert. Most plants have adapted to be able to hold on to what water they have, wait for long periods between rains, and respond quickly when water does become available. However, another factor, the intense heat, makes holding on to water, or surviving without it, much harder.

FINDING WATER

Desert plants can usually be found in predictable places. One common spot is along the edges of dry riverbeds. Water from recent floods may linger in the deeper soils built up from previous floods. This is also the most likely place where water will flow after a rain. Animals like coyotes know this. They will often dig holes in dry riverbeds to find water.

Many creatures have learned to take advantage of the short periods when pools of standing water form after rains. Protozoa (single-celled organisms) reproduce in these pools, then they form a tough coating that holds moisture inside their bodies when the pool dries up. They spend the rest of the year lying dormant in the dry soil. Small shrimp, crabs, and water fleas also breed quickly in these pools before dying or going dormant. Insects, especially beetles, are very successful at surviving in the desert. Most of them have hard shells with a waxy, waterproof layer to hold moisture in their bodies.

Plants and animals in coastal deserts are adapted to collect moisture from fog. Some coastal desert plants have hairs that can capture and hold large amounts of condensed dew. The body of the fog-catching beetle in the Namib Desert, for example, is shaped to funnel water to the insect's mouth.

DESERT PLANTS

Desert heat can quickly sap the moisture from both plants and animals. Temperatures can be so hot for so long that water will simply evaporate from the surface of—and even from within—plants' leaves. A common strategy for dealing with the scarcity of water is to be inactive for much of the year. Many species of desert plants spend most of their lives as seeds, waiting for enough water so they can grow. They spend only a few weeks out of the year as mature plants.

During the long dry periods, desert plants' seeds stay moist and viable because they are covered with a waxy coating that holds in moisture and prevents desiccation or drying out. After a heavy rainstorm, the waxy coatings dissolve. The seeds then germinate, grow into plants, flower, and form new seeds very quickly. Before the plant dries out, the seeds drop to the ground and spend the next dry period near the surface, waiting for the next rain.

Having smaller leaves helps plants conserve water. The smaller the surface area of the leaf, the less water will be lost. The leaves of many desert plants also have waxy coatings or hairs that help them hold on to water.

Another strategy plants use to avoid the heat is to lose their leaves in times of drought. They stop photosynthesizing and become dormant. These kinds of plants are called deciduous. Unlike temperate deciduous plants, which lose their leaves once a year, deciduous plants of the desert can grow as many as four or five batches of leaves in a year as water becomes available. The brittlebush of North American deserts grows different leaves depending upon weather conditions. In dry periods, smaller, hairy leaves help conserve and hold water. After rains, larger leaves grow to increase photosynthesis.

Brittlebush, a member of the sunflower family common in desert environments, gets its name from its easily broken stems.

Succulents are successful desert plants, because they can store water in their fleshy leaves. For example, succulents like aloes and agaves have long, thick, fleshy leaves.

Some plants get around the leaf problem by not having any. Cacti, such as saguaro and barrel cactus of the Sonoran Desert, store water in their stems, and they have spines instead of leaves. The stiff, pointed spines are light in color and help to reflect light away from the cacti. The spines also catch a lot of dew in coastal fog deserts. Most other plants photosynthesize with their leaves, but cacti produce carbohydrates using their stems.

Cacti provide food for many desert creatures. Bats, bees, and other insects feed on the flowers' nectar, while deer, mice, and other mammals eat the fruits.

Cacti also can produce "rain roots." These temporary roots grow within hours of rain, spread out just under the soil surface, and absorb whatever water they can. They dry out and die back when the soil dries out.

MAMMALS AND BIRDS

Mammals and birds are endothermic, or warm-blooded. They create their own heat with a very active metabolism. But this means that they have to eat often to maintain these high metabolisms and high body temperatures.

Many desert mammals survive without ever drinking water. They rely on their own metabolism to keep their bodies hydrated, or moist. Some animals receive most of their moisture from the food they eat. Carnivores, like hawks, owls, and foxes, absorb moisture from the bodies of their prey. However, they have to eat more than they need just to get enough water. A coyote will even eat succulents to add water to its diet.

Most desert predators, such as this falcon, get most of their moisture from the prey they eat.

31

Other creatures will escape to underground burrows in the heat of the day. Rodents, such as pocket mice, prairie dogs, and kangaroo rats, may have extensive networks of tunnels beneath the desert's surface. The temperature in these tunnels can be very cool and comfortable. Rodents are seed-eaters and use their underground burrows to store seeds. This not only ensures that they will have food for the leaner times of drought, when plants are not producing seeds, but it also keeps their food moist. When the mice are hiding out from the sun in their burrows, the water vapor given off by their breath is absorbed by the seeds. When the mice eat the seeds, they are reabsorbing that extra moisture.

Some mammals have adapted so that they can be in the sun for longer periods of time. The Cape ground squirrel from the Kalahari Desert in Africa is able to spend more time out in the sun looking for food because of its long, bushy tail. When the tail is raised and curled over the squirrel's body, its body temperature drops by 9 °F (5 °C).

Large desert mammals such as camels, goats, and donkeys have a thick coat of hair on their backs. Instead of making them hotter, this layer actually insulates them from the heat. The outer layer of hair on a camel may reach 158 °F (70 °C), while the animal's body temperature remains a normal 104 °F (40 °C). These animals also have very little hair on their undersides, which helps them release heat.

Their tails shade ground squirrels from the heat of the desert sun. In especially hot weather, these squirrels lie in the shade and flick sand onto their backs to keep cool.

Nonetheless, large mammals generate a lot of heat. They need to keep their brains cool or they will die. Their bodies keep their brains cool by passing the blood through a network of blood vessels in the back of their necks. This cools the blood before it enters the brain.

Contrary to popular belief, camels do not store water in their humps. A camel's hump is actually a store of fat, which aids them in releasing heat from their bodies as well as serving as an energy source. However, camels are known for their ability to store water in their bodies and to go for long periods without drinking. Donkeys can also store water; they can survive for more than a week without drinking.

Most desert animals conserve water internally by reabsorbing it from their urine before it leaves their bodies. The urine that they do pass is concentrated.

Birds deal with the dry periods by flying away. They find water elsewhere and return after rains to take advantage of the brief flurry of new life—flowers, seeds, and the offspring of insects or rodents.

The letter-winged kite, a species of raptor, flies around the deserts of Australia, following the rains and more importantly, following long-haired rats, one of their major food sources. Long-haired rat populations increase after rains, and if there are plentiful rains and rats, the kites will raise more than one brood of young in a season. If there is a years-long drought, the kites will not breed at all.

REPTILES AND AMPHIBIANS

Reptiles and amphibians are ectothermic, or cold-blooded. They absorb heat from their environment. Ectotherms have slower metabolisms than mammals and have to maintain a body temperature of 100 °F (38 °C) through their behavior.

Lizards will move into the sun in the morning, usually onto a rock, to warm themselves after a cool night. When they become too hot, they

Spadefoot toads emerge from their burrows after rainstorms, ready to mate and lay their eggs in rainwater pools.

will find a shady spot. If no shade is available, lizards will stand on their claws, holding their bodies as far away from the ground as possible, to lessen the amount of heat absorbed.

Several species of spadefoot toad spend the time between rains beneath the ground. They will burrow into moist soil down to 3 feet (1 m) deep. Once at a comfortable level, the toads' metabolism slows down, and they form a tough, leathery outer layer of skin to help hold moisture. They may spend months at a time in this state. When the rains saturate the soil above them, the toads awaken and dig their way to the surface, where they shed their skins. They quickly mate and lay their eggs in the temporary pools formed by the rains.

Desert tortoises spend the dry season hibernating in burrows. They can store a lot of water in their bodies and, if necessary, will urinate on themselves to cool down. As the liquid evaporates off their skin, it draws heat with it, cooling the tortoise's body.

INSECTS

In temperate deserts, insects are mostly diurnal, or active during the day. In hot deserts, insects are nocturnal, or active at night.

Desert locusts live on their own during dry periods. When rains come to a particular area, they swarm together, changing their appearance and habits. They do this to feed on the flush of plant growth where the rains occur. They also like to lay their eggs in moist soil. When the rains disperse, they revert once again to their solitary lives.

Darkling beetles of the Namib Desert actually create their own small weather systems to keep themselves cool. Since their hard outer shells are black, they absorb heat from the sun. The shells heat the air at the surface, which causes the air to rise. The rising air provides a vacuum that pulls in cooler air to replace it.

This darkling beetle's long hind legs raise its rear end above its head, so rainwater can flow down its back and into its mouth.

The most numerous by far of all desert insects are termites and ants. They live below ground in communal nests, and don't spend much time out in the heat. They spend their time feeding in logs of yucca trees or in piles of dung.

HUMANS IN THE DESERTS

Like other mammals, humans are endothermic and are not particularly well adapted to life in the desert. However, many people do live in or near desert regions.

Overheating is a very real danger to people living in hot climates. Moving around a lot in the intense heat of the day can lead to hyperthermia, or dangerously high body temperatures. This can lead to heat exhaustion, heat stroke, or death. To help combat this problem, blood vessels in the body dilate, or expand, allowing blood to flow to the arms and legs, away from the body's core. Heat is more easily lost this way.

Sweating also helps to cool the body. Compared with other mammals, humans who live in desert climates are fortunate that their bodies are mostly hairless. All that exposed skin allows sweat to dry up quickly in a process called evaporative cooling. Since the human body is two-thirds water, people living in the desert have to worry most about dehydration and salt loss. If a person drinks enough water, they can stay active for longer periods of time in desert heat.

Like some desert animals, human urine will become concentrated when people are dehydrated. While this helps to conserve water, it also alters the balance of fluids in the body. Salts are more concentrated, and the body releases them with the urine and sweat. This means that it is necessary for a dehydrated person to take in salt as well as water to restore the balance of these substances in the body. If a person drinks water too quickly without also taking in salt, he or she can get heat cramps.

Camels are well adapted to the hot desert climate. Humans, such as this Bedouin, have to wear loose-fitting clothes, which keep the sun off their skin and allow air to flow.

Interestingly, people who are born and spend the first two years of their lives in hot climates develop a greater number of active sweat glands than people born in temperate climates. Adults from other climates can become somewhat adapted to the desert heat, but not as well as someone born there. They may sweat more to enhance their cooling, and their sweat may be more dilute, conserving salts in the body.

Wearing clothes in the desert can actually keep a person cooler. Loose-fitting, breathable clothes keep the sun from hitting the skin, which reduces the chance of sunburn. Clothes also keep the body cool by preventing the warmer air from coming in contact with the skin.

A loose weave of cotton clothing also allows sweat to freely evaporate from the skin, while preventing excessive water loss. As much as 1 cup (0.25 liter) less water is lost from a clothed body through sweat than a naked body. This is why the Bedouin people of Northern Africa wear long robes.

Spring colors in the Sonoran Desert.

4

HOT DESERTS

Hot deserts occur throughout the world and cover about 14 percent of Earth's land surface. Examples include the Sahara and Kalahari Deserts in Africa; the Arabian Desert; the Thar Desert in northwestern India; the Australian deserts; and the Mojave, Sonoran, and Chihuahuan Deserts of North America. The Atacama Desert in Chile and Peru, South America, is considered both a hot desert and a coastal desert. Hot deserts include some of the driest places on the planet, such as the central Sahara. Some locations receive virtually no rain at all for many years. In one twenty-year span in the last half of the twentieth century, the city of Antofagasta in the Atacama Desert received no rain at all for seventeen of those years.

When rainstorms do occur, they are usually sudden and violent, dropping many inches of water in a very short period. Twenty inches (500 mm) of rain was recorded in one twenty-four-hour period in the Thar Desert.

Air temperatures in hot deserts can reach a maximum of 113 to 117 °F (45 to 47 °C). The highest temperature ever recorded is 136 °F (58 °C) in the Libyan Desert in September 1922.

Soil temperatures can be even hotter, with 172 °F (78 °C) recorded at the soil surface in the Sahara. However, temperatures become much less severe just several inches below the soil's surface. In Israel's Negev Desert, at a depth of 20 inches (50 cm) soil temperatures between 57 and 77 °F (14 and 25 °C) were recorded. At 39 inches (1 m), temperatures were measured at a cool 68 °F (20 °C). This haven from the hot sun is beneficial for burrowing animals as well as for the roots and bulbs of plants.

Since hot deserts have fewer scattered plants than temperate deserts, winds blow more freely across their open landscape. The nearly constant winds also help form and change the shape of sand dunes. Hot, dry

HOT DESERTS

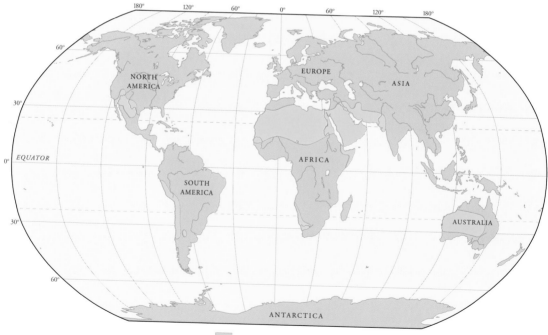

Main regions of hot deserts

winds blow in regular seasons. Khamsin winds scatter the sand of Middle Eastern deserts from May to October. Santa Ana winds build from October through March in the southwestern United States and blow all the way out to the Pacific coast. In addition to these regular winds, more intense winds may suddenly form, spawning dust storms that block all visibility, damage vegetation, and erode landforms.

SAHARA

Nearly the size of the entire United States of America, the Sahara Desert is by far the largest desert on Earth. Its 3.5 million square miles (9 million km²) encompass most of northern Africa within ten different countries.

The hottest and driest climate occurs in the deep center of the desert, where temperatures can reach 130 °F (55 °C) in the shade. In winter, the northern edges of the Sahara may experience hoar frost, which forms on the ground from dew. Harmattan winds are intense winds that kick up dense dust storms in the southern region.

Algeria's Great Eastern Erg is one of the many sand seas that cover nearly one-third of the Sahara. Ancient caravan routes that carried many desert travelers across the great expanse lie on rockier ground between the shifting sand dunes.

Mountains within the Sahara are tall enough that their cooler climates support plants similar to those seen in the chaparral and scrub biome. Some of these mountains are volcanically active.

Formerly a wetter region of grasslands, savannas, and woodlands, the Sahara began to dry up again about 8,000 years ago. Many of the animals and plants from that time died out as the climate became hotter and drier, and humans hunted many large animals to extinction. Current plant life of the Sahara is very limited, with only about 500 species known.

Animals of the Sahara

Animal life of the Sahara is more diverse than might be expected, based on the harsh conditions and low diversity of plants. Many species of reptiles, birds, and mammals call the Sahara home.

The desert eagle owl hunts the northern region of the Sahara, preying upon a wide range of animals, including beetles, lizards, snakes, foxes, and even small antelope. Ranging over most of the Sahara, the desert hedgehog lives in burrows during the day and feeds on scorpions, frogs, and insects after sunset. This creature is known for curling up in a spiny ball to fend off predators.

The world's smallest wild cat, the sand cat, occupies the northern region of the Sahara, as well as desert regions in Arabia and Central Asia. It digs shallow tunnels in which it spends the day. The sand cat feeds, like many desert predators, on almost anything, including insects and birds, but it prefers rodents like gerbils. Its wide feet and small size allow the sand cat to move easily across the sand without sinking.

A large, light-colored antelope, the addax formerly ranged

The sand cat, from the deserts of northern Africa and the Arabian Peninsula, can hear the faint movements of gerbils beneath the sand with its large ears. It then digs in the sand to find its prey.

The addax digs beds in the sand, usually in the shade of shrubs or boulders, to escape the heat and strong winds of the Sahara Desert.

widely over the Sahara Desert. Now it only exists in isolated populations in the north and is threatened with extinction.

Humans in the Sahara

The arid Sahara region does not support any significant farming or ranching communities. Most of the settled human population is centered around the rivers that flow through the desert. The Nile and the Niger are the two largest rivers, and several smaller rivers supply and drain Lake Chad.

Oil and minerals are the main riches drawn from the Sahara Desert. Libya and Algeria have a large supply of oil and natural gas, while Tunisia, Mauritania, and Morocco profit from mining phosphates, which are used as plant fertilizer.

Many people have proposed developing solar power in the Sahara. The intense sun beating down constantly on the desert would be able to provide a bountiful and renewable source of energy. This energy source would be much cleaner and less environmentally harmful than oil and gas extraction. Unfortunately, solar power technology is not currently advanced enough to make such a project profitable.

The Sahara is populated by three major groups of people, Arabs, Berber, and Tuareg. The oldest group is the Berber, and their true origins are unknown. The Berbers still maintain their culture and live both in the Atlas Mountains as farmers and nomadically throughout the desert. But many of these people were displaced as Arab armies moved in from the Middle East in the seventh century, bringing the Islamic religion with them. Today, the Arabs are the largest group in the northern Sahara.

The Tuareg, a nomadic people who have roamed the desert for centuries, may be descended from the Berbers. Approximately one million Tuaregs raise cattle, camels, goats, and sheep. These people follow the water, moving their herds from place to place, wherever rains have recently fallen or wherever seasonal water is available.

NORTH AMERICA

North America is an incredibly diverse continent, and is comprised of as many as six different biomes. Different habitat types fade into one another, forming a patchwork of plant and animal life amidst different geologies and climates.

The southwest corner of North America is largely dominated by the desert biome. Grasslands and shrublands grow along the edges of arid deserts, intermingled with forested mountains. The area is large and diverse and contains three distinct desert formations.

Mojave

The Mojave Desert lies in the states of California, Nevada, and Arizona. Its arid climate is caused by the rain shadow effect of the Sierra Nevada Mountains and the coastal range of California. The Mojave is very dry and is home to the hottest location in North America, Death Valley, which lies at 280 feet (86 m) below sea level.

However, this is not the hottest or the lowest desert on the continent. Most of the Mojave lies at elevations from 1,950 to 3,900 feet (600 to 1,200 m). Winter frosts do occur, with occasional snow at the highest elevations. Rain falls in the winter and can last from several hours to several days at a time.

The Mojave is truly a unique desert. Twenty-five percent of the plant and animal species are endemic, meaning they only live in this

Joshua trees grow only in the Mojave Desert and, like other yucca species, rely upon a single species of moth to pollinate their flowers.

location. One unique plant group, tree yuccas, can grow up to 30 feet (9 m) tall. Joshua trees, one of several species of tree yucca, can be found at high elevations. However, most plants are shrubs. The dominant plant at lower elevations is creosote bush, an aromatic plant with waxy leaves, used by Native Americans for many medicinal purposes.

Sonoran

To the east of the Mojave and wrapping around the Gulf of California is the diverse Sonoran Desert. This international desert straddles the United States-Mexico border from the Baja California peninsula through the states of Arizona and California and down into Sonora.

Larger and more sprawling than the Mojave, the Sonoran Desert has two weather systems. The eastern portion is influenced by the Gulf of California, and any rain that falls does so in summer. Winter rains are the norm in the western portion, which is influenced by moisture from the Pacific Ocean. The center of the desert receives roughly equal rainfall in both seasons. This is truly a hot desert, with warm winters and hot summers.

The Sonoran contains a remarkable diversity of plants. There are many species of small trees, such as acacia, paloverde,

Chollas are one large group of North American cactus. There are twenty-eight species in the state of Arizona alone.

Many birds, including these American kestrels, use holes in large saguaro cacti for nesting and as shelter from the sun.

and ironwood. Succulents take many forms here, such as cholla, which is a branching, shrublike cactus. When the long, sharp spines of this plant snag in fur, clothing, or skin, the fleshy tip of the woody branch breaks away, imbedded in its host. This serves as an effective strategy for reproduction. When this tip falls from its host, it can root into the ground, starting a new cholla bush.

Larger cacti like the saguaro serve as trees in the Sonoran Desert. The Gila woodpecker, the cactus wren, the saw-whet owl, and other birds use holes in the massive central stems for nests or as a shady place to avoid the scorching heat. Saguaros can reach 50 feet in height, but they normally grow roughly 30 feet and have about five branches, or arms. Their beautiful, white, night-blooming flowers attract many insects, birds, and bats. Organ pipe, another large cactus species, grows in huge stands in the southwest corner of Arizona and northern Mexico. A cluster of long, curving, slender stems grows from a single point in the ground to make up one plant.

The ocotillo is a unique, woody desert plant with many long, whip-like branches rooted to the ground. Usually leafless except after rains, the ocotillo flowers and fruits at the beginning of the growing season. The multiple, vibrant, orange-red flowers attract many pollinators.

Sidewinders

Rattlesnakes only occur in North America, and most live in and around the desert Southwest. There are several species common to the deserts, including the western diamondback, black-tailed, and Mojave rattlesnakes.

The sidewinder rattlesnake lives mostly in sandy desert areas with little vegetation. It has adapted to this environment of loose, moving soil, by evolving a particular movement style called sidewinding. Many snakes can move this way, but the sidewinder is particularly adept at it.

By making a loop with its body, then tossing the loop in front of the rest of its body, the snake can use that loop for traction and pull itself along. Doing this continuously allows the sidewinder to move rather quickly, while keeping only a small part of its body in contact with the hot sands.

The sidewinder wiggles and burrows into the sand to avoid the desert heat. It waits here for unsuspecting prey to pass, then it lunges out to sink its fangs in, releasing a deadly poison.

Other species that practice this sidewinding motion occur in other deserts of the world. The horned viper of the Sahara Desert has the same horny points above its eyes as the sidewinder of North America. The Namaqua dwarf adder and Peringuey's adder of the Namib Desert in western Africa are also sidewinders.

A Peringuey's adder

Chihuahuan

Many of the plant and animal species common to the Mojave and the Sonoran Deserts also occur in the Chihuahuan Desert, but overall, the Chihuahuan is the most diverse of the three. It is also the largest North American Desert, covering more than 200,000 square miles (518,000 km²). The Chihuahuan lies mostly on the north central plateau of Mexico, but also stretches north of the border into Arizona, New Mexico, and Texas.

With half of the desert above 3,300 feet (1,000 m) in elevation, the Chihuahuan Desert is subject to greater temperature extremes than the other two North American hot deserts. Freezing temperatures occur at the higher elevations, but the summers are long and hot.

Rain falls in the summer here, but the rain shadows from northern Mexico's two major north-south trending mountain chains—the Sierra Madre Occidental to the west and the Sierra Madre Oriental to the east—keep the Chihuahuan Desert very dry. Rainstorms are short and violent.

Generally, the Chihuahuan Desert is a shrub desert, with few tall plants other than tree yuccas. An unusual feature is the extensive grasslands growing on deeper soils. They may be remnants of a more widespread grassland community. Cacti are even more diverse and abundant here than in the Sonoran Desert.

The southern grasshopper mouse doesn't live in communal groups like other rodents, so it has developed a call to locate others of its own species.

49

The Patagonian cavy, the second largest rodent in the world, makes its home in Patagonian desert grasslands.

5

TEMPERATE DESERTS

Most of the temperate deserts of the world are deep in the interior of large continents. These are arid deserts, far from a major water source, with hot summers and winter temperatures that fall below freezing.

A wide variation of daily temperatures is also common here. Because of the arid climate, the land heats up quickly during the day and loses heat easily at night. In more humid climates, such as the tropics, moisture in the air holds heat close to the ground. Little or no rain falls in temperate deserts during the summer, and dew may be the main source of moisture for long periods. Snow falls in winter and can stay on the ground for several days.

The three main formations of temperate desert are in Eurasia, the western United States, and Patagonia, which is in the South American country of Argentina. The Eurasian formation is vast and by far the largest, stretching from the Caspian and Aral Seas in the west to the Mongolia-China border in the east. The region contains many smaller deserts, including the Taklamakan in China, the Kyzyl Kum in Uzbekistan, the Kara Kum in Turkmenistan, the high valleys of Tibet, and other deserts in Iran, Pakistan, and India. The rainy season varies from winter in the west to summer in the east.

Snow covers the desert soil in Big Bend National Park in Texas.

All temperate deserts occur on plains or plateaus, in areas where large inland seas or lakes once existed. These bodies of water have left behind clay and silt sediments, fine-textured soils that keep rainwater from seeping into the ground. (Hot deserts have larger proportions of sand and gravel, which absorb water more readily.) Water pools on these surfaces and slowly evaporates, leaving behind salts.

Large areas of exposed rock also keep water from absorbing into the ground. Sand fields are much less common in temperate deserts than in hot deserts, but dune fields do occur where ancient beaches or river deltas existed, mostly in Eurasia.

The climate extremes can be so severe in these deserts that the diversity of plants is poor. Since very little water actually penetrates the soil, plants have to rely upon the rain and melting winter snow that has worked its way underground through cracks and other openings. Shrubs are more common in these deserts, because their deeper roots can reach this moisture more easily than shallow-rooted herbs.

Most of the plants in the Patagonian Desert are very different than those found in the other temperate deserts. This is probably because South America has been isolated from the other continents for a very long time.

Animals in the three major temperate desert formations are very different. However, many animals have evolved similar forms and occupy similar ecological niches, or places in nature. This type of development is known as parallel evolution. For example, two different species of plant-eating tortoise occur in the warmer regions of both the North American and Eurasian formations.

TEMPERATE DESERTS

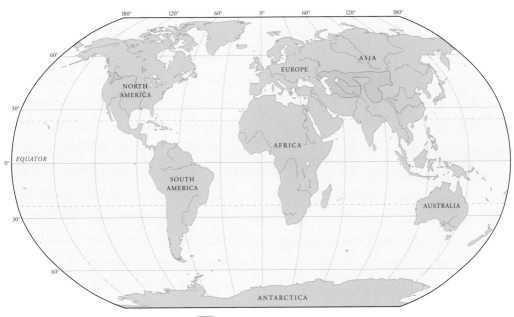

Main regions of temperate deserts

GREAT BASIN

The name "Great Basin" conjures up images of a huge bathtub. In reality, the Great Basin Desert in North America is not one but many flat basins, or depressions, amidst mountains and mountain ranges. Geologists call this type of landscape "basin and range." Rain falling on the mountains drains into these basins and pools until it evaporates.

The whole region is known as the Great Basin because it lies between two major mountain chains—the Rocky Mountains to the east and the Sierra Nevada and Cascade Mountains to the west. The Great Basin is the largest desert in the United States. The Sierra-Cascade range, running through Washington, Oregon, and California, forms a rain shadow that keeps Pacific Ocean moisture from reaching this parched land. The Rockies hold back moisture from Great Plains storms to the east.

Moisture in the form of snow is abundant on the high peaks of the Sierra Nevada Mountains, but little falls on Death Valley, the desert to the east of the mountains.

Rivers have cut deep canyons in the easily eroded sedimentary rock, channeling water and floods. As a result, this water is mostly unavailable to the plants growing on the higher plateaus. Loose soils moved around by the rivers are also hemmed in, preventing them from being blown around by winds and collected into sand dunes.

This region started forming in the Cretaceous Period (144 to 65 million years ago) by a series of major earthquakes and volcanoes. The land rose to the west, forming the mountain ranges along the western coast. Over millions of years, huge amounts of sediment, or loose soil, washed to the east, filling this basin.

Temperate desert plants are mostly grasses and shrubs, such as sagebrush and saltbrush. These plants have dense evergreen leaves that contain aromatic oils, much like chaparral plants. These oily, tough leaves resist drying out in the hot, windy climate. Very few cactus species grow in the Great Basin Desert.

People of the Great Basin

Historically, various nomadic Native American groups roamed the region, including Navajo, Ute, and Shoshone. Miners were some of the first white settlers to explore the area, and Mormons soon followed, looking to settle in a place free from religious persecution. Many mining boom towns cropped up after the California Gold Rush of the mid-nineteenth century, but these did not last long.

The Mormons, however, developed a long-lasting settlement after many years of difficulties. They soon spread across the West, establishing villages and farms wherever they found water.

With so much open space and few laws, many settlers took possession of land, displacing the Native peoples. Forests were cut and many animals were killed without regard to the health of the land. Over the past 150 years, cattle grazing has caused a gradual change in plant cover from grasses and herbs to shrubs. Now only about 10 percent of the original

55

Great Basin vegetation remains. Neither livestock nor native wildlife, such as pronghorn antelope and mule deer, will eat most of the shrubs.

Fire, not historically common in the Great Basin, has become more prevalent because of the introduction of more fire-prone, nonnative plant species. The region's native annuals—herbs which die back and

Living Soil

In the deserts of the world, surface soils tend to be dry with sparsely scattered vegetation. Sometimes cyanobacteria, lichen, algae, fungi, and mosses will spread out between plants, binding the soil together into a living mat or crust. The rootlike structures of these plants hold soil in place on steep slopes and in other places where wind and water would normally carry it away. The crust also keeps the soil moist long after rains have fallen. In the intervening dry periods, the crust organisms exist in a desiccated state, but they are able to come alive again when the next rains come.

Since these crusts are better able to hold water than the soil is, they provide sites where plants can live in an otherwise hostile environment. Many desert plants take root in these mats not only for the moisture the crusts provide, but also for essential nutrients they find there.

These vital, life-giving crusts, while resilient against heat and drought, are nonetheless easily destroyed. Herds of cattle that roam widely across many deserts often trample and compact the soil. Humans traveling by foot or vehicle also damage the crust. With nothing to hold it in place, the soil is easily blown away by winds or washed away by the infrequent heavy rains. This eroded soil can cover and smother other crust areas.

re-sprout every year—have been replaced by these plants that were imported accidentally and also planted intentionally. One of these exotic plants, cheatgrass brome, burns much more easily than native plants and spreads rapidly after fires. The more cheatgrass there is, the more likely it is that an area will burn. Once the area has burned, other non-native species can sprout, further changing the makeup of the landscape.

GOBI

The Gobi Desert is a vast, arid desert of 500,000 square miles (1,295,000 km²) in southern Mongolia and northern China, comprising several distinct arid regions.

The word gobi *is Mongolian for "waterless place."*

The arid conditions of the Gobi are created by the Himalayan Mountains and the Tibetan Plateau to the south, which form a rain shadow that shields the desert from Indian Ocean moisture.

The Taklamakan Desert lies in the Tarim Basin, a long bowl-shaped depression in the western part of the Gobi, and is surrounded on three sides by towering mountain ranges. This is a very empty region of salt-encrusted, dry lakebeds among sand dunes and low hills. The lowest elevation at the center of the basin is 500 feet (154 m) below sea level.

In the Taklamakan, there is a wide range of temperatures—as much as 86 °F (30 °C) from winter to summer and 68 °F (20 °C) from day to night. As little as 0.5 inches (1.25 cm) of rain falls in a year. Most of the desert is composed of mobile sand dunes, and intense sandstorms are common in April and May.

Plants are sparsely scattered across the dry, shifting sands of the Taklamakan. Most common are tamarisk, dwarf willows, and grasses in low areas where water collects.

More plants can be found in the grasslands, or steppes, that lie on the edges of the Gobi and in the eastern deserts, including the Ordus Desert and the Alashan Desert along the Mongolian border with China. The climate is less dry and severe here than in the Taklamakan. Groundwater is closer to the surface, and oases are more common.

Animals of the Gobi

A variety of animals make the Gobi Desert their home. The takhi, or Przewalski's horse has never been domesticated. The species went extinct in the wild in the 1960s. Fortunately, enough were still alive in captivity in zoos that they could be bred and reintroduced into the wild.

A wild population of the Bactrian camel also roams the Gobi. These two-humped camels are descendants of the breed that was domesticated more than 4,000 years ago. The khulan is a more widespread hoofed mammal of the Gobi, with herds of 500 or more roaming the plateau. Also

Two ancestral lines gave birth to today's horses. All the domesticated horses of the world descended from one line, while Przewalski's horses, from Mongolia, represent the other line.

known as the wild ass, the khulan can run as fast as 40 miles (65 km) an hour.

The golden eagle, a large raptor common throughout the world, soars the skies above the Gobi, scanning among the sparse vegetation for jerboas—small, long-eared rodents that live in burrows. Jerboas have evolved strong, long hind legs for jumping to avoid the many predators that hunt them.

There are more than 2 million domesticated Bactrian camels in the world, but only about 950 wild camels still roam the deserts and steppes of China and Mongolia. The wild Bactrian camel is considered critically endangered.

People of the Gobi

Despite the harsh conditions, many people have traveled through the region for thousands of years along the ancient Silk Road. Actually several different routes connecting oases, the Silk Road was a major trade route between the east and west for transporting gold and other precious metals, stones, glass, animals, plants, and even ideas and religious beliefs. Most routes skirted the edges of the barren Taklamakan Desert.

In the western region of the Gobi, Khalkha Mongols, a nomadic people, have been herding the two-humped Bactrian camels from oasis to oasis for thousands of years. These camels are well suited to the desert climate, able to endure the dry conditions and extreme temperatures. The camels transport the Mongols' goods as well as provide wool for clothing, while sheep and goats are herded for meat and for wool.

Nomadic Mongolians travel with their animal herds between water sources, carrying their gers, or round tents, with them. These tents are very easy to set up, break down, and transport.

Flowers bloom on foothills in the Atacama Desert of Chile, below the towering Andes Mountains.

6

COASTAL DESERTS

While they exist in the hot and dry horse latitudes, coastal deserts are different enough from hot deserts to be put in a category all their own. All coastal deserts occur on the west coasts of land masses. They are influenced by their proximity to oceans, and fog is a major water source. The four formations of coastal desert are in Baja California in western Mexico, on the island nation of Madagascar, in Chile, and in western Africa.

Temperature ranges in coastal deserts are not as great as in other desert types. Cool winters and warm summers are more common. These deserts are very dry, with only 3 to 5 inches (8 to 13 cm) of rain per year.

It may seem odd for a desert to be so close to an ocean. All that moisture should be good for coastal areas. However, these deserts exist because northerly ocean winds move along the coast, carrying away most moisture before it reaches land.

Most of the moisture these deserts receive is in the form of fog. When the cold ocean water meets the warm air, water vapor forms. As the fog moves inland and upslope, moisture condenses as a heavy dew and coats soil, plants, and animals.

NAMIB

The oldest desert in the world, the Namib Desert, stretches 1,200 miles (1,900 km) in a narrow strip along the west coast of Africa in Namibia and Angola. Within this 20- to 90-mile-wide (30- to 140-km-wide) strip are desert sands lining the Atlantic Ocean, dry riverbeds, gravel beds, miles-long linear dunes, and jagged mountains reaching up to the Great Escarpment. This is the long series of mountain ranges that encircles the southern tip of Africa. The Namib Desert's position between the ocean and the Great Escarpment have isolated it from other ecosystems, allowing unique species of plants and animals to evolve.

Coastal Region

Winds sweep northward along the Atlantic coast of Africa for most of the year, moving surface water along with them. An upwelling of cold, nutrient-rich water, known as the Benguela Current, rises from the deep ocean to take the place of the surface water. The cold Benguela Current provides moisture for life on land. For more than half the year, morning fog forms when warm air meets the cold water of the ocean. As the fog is blown inland, it condenses as dew on soils, plants, and animals.

Dwarf shrubs grow in a narrow strip between the coast and the dune fields in the northern half of the desert. Farther inland from the ocean, the fog's effects decrease. Temperatures are hotter by day and cooler by night, and more rain falls.

The relatively few bird species that live in the Namib are found along the coast, where they feed on the abundant food in the ocean and in

If a wheel spider from the Namibian Desert senses danger, it quickly tucks in its legs and rolls its body down a dune to escape.

coastal ponds. Birds such as the dune lark, Benguela long-billed lark, bank cormorant, and tractrac chat are found nowhere else in the world.

Dunes

Linear dunes compose most of the southern region of the Namib, running in north-south lines up to 30 miles (48 km) long. Younger dunes closer to the coast are composed of yellow sand. Farther east the dunes gradually change color from yellow-brown to brown to brick red, which is caused by a buildup of iron oxide. One of the world's largest groupings of star dunes exists in the northern region of the desert.

Wind-blown plant matter and dead insects accumulate on the leeward side of dunes. This food source supports groups of animals, including beetles and other insects, that provide food for lizards, which are then eaten by snakes. Roughly seventy species of reptiles live in the Namib Desert.

The Namib is also unusually rich in beetle species, especially in the darkling beetle family. They easily burrow into the dunes to avoid heat and detection by predators. Fifty species of these clever beetles have evolved to take advantage of dew as a water source.

The body casing of the fog-basking or head-standing beetle is shaped to funnel water to its mouth. It perches on the coastal-facing dunes, raises the back of its body, and waits for the dew to condense into water. When it does, the water rolls down the beetle's back and into its mouth. The fog-trapping beetle digs a trench to capture dew, which it then drinks.

Gerbils, moles, bats, and other small rodents live in various habitats in the Namib. Many of them tunnel into the sand to escape predators and the heat.

Rivière

Dry riverbeds, known as *rivière*, are common in the north. Although winter rains only fill the *rivière* for a few days or even hours at a time,

Klipspringers jump nimbly among rocks in the Namib Desert and nearby grasslands. Its feet are so small that the antelope can stand on a spot the size of a silver dollar.

they are still able to support grasses, shrubs, and trees such as acacia and wild tamarisk.

Many mammals congregate along the riverbeds, where vegetation and occasional water can be found. Here, cheetahs, leopards, hyenas, and foxes hunt larger prey—klipspringers and steenboks and other hoofed mammals—that come to the riverbeds for food and water.

Gravel Fields

Colorful lichens cover the gravel fields in the north. In the eastern section of these gravel fields, seeds of grasses lie dormant in the soils. When rains come, they quickly sprout, suddenly changing the landscape into a grassland.

Also among the gravel plains, the strange Welwitschia plants grow in shallow channels that funnel rainwater from higher ground. These ancient plants can live to be 2,500 years old and are only found in the Namib Desert. Their 5-foot-long (1.5 m), heavy, straplike leaves curl into unusual shapes aboveground, while their root systems can extend 98 feet (30 m) below ground.

Welwitschia plants are able to survive in these channels because water from floods seeps about 3 feet (1 m) down into the soil and can

The leaves of Welwitschia plants are never shed, but continue to grow from the base, like grasses. These plants can live between 400 and 1,500 years.

stay there for years. They are also one of the few plants that can absorb moisture though their leaves, an important talent in a region where nearly all the moisture comes from fog.

ATACAMA

Chile's Atacama Desert has been called the driest place on Earth. It stretches for more than 600 miles (1,000 km) south from southern Peru into Chile between the Pacific Ocean in the west and the towering Andes Mountains in the east. Within this 60-mile-wide (100-km-wide) strip, the desert rises from beach to a dry plateau that reaches a maximum elevation of 4,900 feet (1,500 m).

As with the Namib Desert, the Atacama's arid climate is caused by offshore winds. In this case, the Humboldt Current, carrying cold

Despite its closeness to the ocean, the Atacama Desert is one of the driest places on Earth.

water north from the Antarctic, is pulled along by these winds. In the summer, almost no rain falls because the heat from the desert evaporates the ocean moisture before it can condense as rain. However, in the winter, the cold ocean water meeting the warm southeast trade winds creates fogs, locally called *camanchaca,* which can penetrate inland because the land is cooler.

The northern coastal region is very dry, and only cactus species grow, some very large and barrel-shaped. Years pass without rain. When the rains do fall, about every five to twelve years, the dormant seeds of herbs sprout. The sand fields are flush with green during the short time needed for the plants to complete their life cycle.

The *camanchaca* only benefit the hills near the southern coast up to an elevation of about 3,250 feet (1,000 m). Islands of vegetation, known as *lomas,* grow amid the dry sandy hills and include grasses, ferns, cacti, and woody plants, many of which are endemics.

Epiphytic plants grow in colonies on bare soil in the *lomas,* but they are not rooted in the ground. These air plants survive largely on the dew moisture they collect. Winds roll these unrooted plants like tumbleweeds across the desert until they become caught among rocks or other plants, where they will reproduce and develop new colonies.

Two species of fox and a vampire bat can be found among the *lomas* communities. Birds such as hummingbirds only visit when plants are in bloom. Other birds, including the Pacific blue-black grassquit, visit to feed on the pupae of insects that hatch at the beginning of winter.

High above the *lomas,* the ocean air continues to rise upslope. It gradually cools, allowing rain or snow to fall at elevations above 9,750 feet (3,000 m). The zone between the fogs and rains, however, is dry and mostly lifeless. This region is not flat but is composed of rolling hills and *quebradas,* or river gorges, where soil and water collects. These are the only places where plants will grow in this zone. Animals are equally scarce. There are only a few species of scorpions, insects, lizards, and rodents.

Mining is the primary human use of the Atacama. Products include copper, iodine salts, and sodium chloride. The practices involved in extracting these minerals, as well as road building and human settlement, are causing untold damage to the delicate ecosystems of the Atacama Desert.

Copper mines are a boon to Chile's economy but a blight on the ecology of the Atacama Desert.

Conclusion

SO HARSH, YET SO DELICATE

Deserts are not hospitable places for any life-form. Most plants and animals that live in these extreme environments have adapted to the heat and aridity over a long period of time.

Humans' historical use of deserts has been mostly to pass from one location to another, going either through the desert or to oases within the desert. People have usually settled on the margins of the desert, in steppes, or grasslands. Not until more recent times have people found uses for the interiors of deserts. Discovery of resources such as oil, minerals, and even water beneath deserts has encouraged people to settle in what was once thought of as an unlivable environment.

Water is obviously a scarce resource in all the world's deserts. Human communities, such as those on the Arabian Peninsula, on the edges of the Namib Desert, and in the Great Plains and Great Basin of the United States, have discovered large underground aquifers. Water is being drawn from these underground reservoirs as if it were unlimited. Unfortunately, the water levels are dropping, causing problems for the human communities that have grown up around them, as well as for desert plants and animals.

Deserts can also spread—with the human "help." Since the grasslands on the edges of many deserts do receive water and have rich soils, they can be used for farming. However, in some areas, crops are irrigated with water from springs, wells, and streams that are rich in salts. When the water evaporates, it leaves a layer of salt, which builds with each watering of the crops in a process called salinization. This makes more and more land unsuitable for any plant growth, cultivated or wild.

Removal of native vegetation for firewood, building materials, or to replace with crops also adds to the process of desertification. If these things are done during times of drought, the problem becomes much worse. A combination of these factors, in addition to a civil war, caused widespread famine in Ethiopia in the 1970s and 1980s. More than one million people starved to death. Desertification continues to affect many millions of people around the world.

Recent discoveries of large aquifers beneath Saudi Arabia's desert lands have made farming methods like this center-pivot-irrigated field in Najd possible. Unfortunately, water is being drawn from these underground sources at an unsustainable rate.

Desert regions are often abused because they are commonly seen as wastelands, fit only for uses that people do not want anywhere else, such as military bases. Weapons testing, including nuclear devices, is commonly done in desert regions. The United States has tested nuclear weapons both above- and belowground in the Great Basin Desert in Nevada. The Lop Nor region in the eastern Taklamakan Desert contains the largest nuclear weapons testing facility in the world and has been used for testing for thirty years.

Many deserts are not well protected because most people don't know or understand how fragile they are. The Atacama Desert is rapidly being exploited for its mineral wealth, and only a few small places exist as protected areas. These range in size from the 12-square-mile (30-km²) La Chimba National Reserve to the Pampa del Tamarugal National Reserve, at 395 square miles (1,023 km²).

However, some countries have set aside larger areas of desert for protection. Namibia has protected 19,216 square miles (49,768 km²) of the Namib Desert in the Namib-Naukluft National Park. Much of the park is off-limits to people because of its fragile nature.

While large areas of the Sonoran Desert have been set aside for protection, such as

Deserts are the preferred sites for nuclear testing, because they are often far from human settlement and assumed to be lifeless.

Arizona's Organ Pipe Cactus National Monument BiosphereReserve, the area suffers from a lack of connection between these protected areas. Roads and development divide them, creating barriers to wildlife movement. Development on bajadas, rocky areas, and along rivers has reduced habitat for many endemic species.

The most important way to protect these fragile ecosystems is through knowledge and awareness. Education about the amazing and delicate life-forms that inhabit these deserts can open people's eyes. They will hopefully recognize the unique position deserts hold at the extremes of life's ability to survive.

Organ Pipe Cactus National Monument contains some of the richest examples of the Sonoran Desert and is designated a World Biosphere Reserve.

GLOSSARY

alluvium—Soil, gravel, and rocks carried by mountain streams and deposited in piles where the stream empties into an open plain; common feature in deserts.

arid—Lack of moisture; describes a region or climate with little rain.

arroyo—A dry riverbed or deep gully cut by an intermittent stream.

butte—An isolated, tall, steep hill with a flat top, often composed of sedimentary rock often topped by a harder rock layer.

cyanobacteria—One-celled or many-celled bacteria; some are aquatic and some live within biological soil crusts in deserts.

desiccation—Drying out completely.

epiphyte—A plant that grows on soil, rocks, buildings, or other plants only for support; it derives its nutrition and moisture from the air.

hoar frost—Frozen dew.

leeward—The direction the wind is blowing: the leeward side of a hill is protected from the wind; opposite of windward.

parallel evolution—Different organisms developing similar characteristics in response to similar environmental pressures.

photosynthesis—The process by which plants produce their own food; the conversion of water and carbon dioxide, with sun as the energy source, into carbohydrates used for growth.

rain shadow—An area that receives little precipitation because a mountain range traps most of the moisture before it can reach it.

salinization—The buildup of salts on soil by the evaporation of rainwater.

sedimentary—Rock composed of compacted sand, silt, and/or clay; usually originally deposited in water.

windward—Facing into the wind; opposite of leeward.

FIND OUT MORE

Books

Allaby, Michael. *Deserts.* New York: Facts on File, 2006.

Johansson, Philip. *The Dry Desert: A Web of Life.* Berkeley Heights, NJ: Enslow Publishers, 2004.

Lawrence, Katherine. *Life in the Desert.* New York: Rosen, 2004.

Web Sites

http://www.desertmuseum.org/
Web site of the Arizona-Sonora Desert Museum, a natural history museum and research facility based in Tucson, Arizona.

http://www.biologicaldiversity.org/swcbd/programs/deserts/
The Center for Biological Diversity's Web site on deserts of the United States.

http://mbgnet.mobot.org/
Designed specifically for kids, this Missouri Botanical Garden Web site describes biomes and ecosystems.

BIBLIOGRAPHY

Allan, Tony, and Andrew Warren. 1993. *Deserts, the Encroaching Wilderness: A World Conservation Atlas.* New York: Oxford University Press.

Andean Botanical Information System. "The Lomas Formations of Coastal Peru: Composition and Biogeographic History." http://www.sacha.org/

Chihuahuan Desert Research Institute, The. "North American Deserts." http://www.cdri.org/index.html

Cowley, Clive. "Journey into Namibia." The Namibian Connection. http://www.orusovo.com/guidebook/default.htm

Evenari, Michael, Imanuel Noy-Meir, David Goodall. 1985. *Ecosystems of the World 12A and 12B: Hot Deserts and Arid Shrublands.* Amsterdam: Elsevier Scientific Publishing Co.

Namibia Online Travel Guide. "Namibia Geography." http://www.namibia-travel.net/index.htm

Newton, Dr. Ian. *Birds of Prey.* San Francisco: Fog City Press, 2000.

Center for Nonproliferation Studies, Monterey Institute of International Studies. "Lop Nor Nuclear Weapons Test Base." The Nuclear Threat Initiative, June, 1998. http://www.nti.org/db/china/lopnur.htm

Online Guide to Namibia, Articles on Flora and Fauna. "Welwitschia Mirabilis." http://www.namibweb.com

Paulson, Dennis. "Biomes of the World." Tacoma, WA: University of Puget Sound, 1997. http://www.ups.edu/biology/museum/worldbiomes.html

Public Broadcasting System. "Sahara." http://www.pbs.org/sahara/index.htm

Public Broadcasting System. "The Living Edens: Namib." http://www.pbs.org/edens/namib/earth.htm

Sahagun, Louis. "In Death Valley, New Life." *Boston Globe.* March 13, 2005.

Southwest Biological Science Center. "Biological Soil Crusts." United States Geological Service, Canyonlands Research Station. http://www.soilcrust.org

Sowell, John. 2001. *Desert Ecology.* Salt Lake City, UT: University of Utah Press.

Thayer, Helen and Bill Thayer. "People of the Wind and Sand: A Trek Across the Gobi Desert." One Earth Adventures. http://www.oneearthadventures.com

University of California, Berkeley Museum of Paleontology. "The World's Biomes." Berkeley, CA: UCMP, 2000. http://www.ucmp.berkeley.edu/glossary/gloss5/biome/

West, Neil E. 1983. *Ecosystems of the World 5: Temperate Deserts and Semi-Deserts.* Amsterdam: Elsevier Scientific Publishing Co.

Whitford, Walter. 2002. *Ecology of Desert Systems.* San Diego: Academic Press.

Wild, Oliver. 1992. "The Silk Road." http://www.ess.uci.edu/~oliver/silk.html

Woodward, Susan L. "Introduction to Biomes." Radford University Geography Department, 1996. http://www.runet.edu/~swoodwar/CLASSES/GEOG235/biomes/intro.html

World Wildlife Fund. "Terrestrial Ecoregions." http://www.worldwildlife.org

INDEX

Page numbers in **boldface** are illustrations.

maps
  Hot Deserts, **40**
  Temperate Deserts, **53**

Africa
  Algerian Sand Sea, 19
  Ethiopian famine, 71
  Kalahari, **13, 26,** 32, **32,
    35, 35,** 39
  Libyan, 39
  Namib, 12, **16,** 17, 18,
    19, 64, 64-67, **66, 67,**
    70, 72
  Sahara, **15,** 41-44, **43,**
    43-44, 48, **48**
alluvium, 17, 23-24
altitude, 58
  See also plateaus
animals, 6-7, **7, 26, 42, 43,**
    48, **48, 49, 50,** 55-56,
    58-59, **59, 60,** 61, **61,**
    66, **66,** 69
  adaptations, 31-36, **32,
    34, 35,** 42, 53, 59
  See also birds; food
  chain; insects
Arabian peninsula.
  See Mideast
arroyos, 14
Asia, 12, 42, 51
  Gobi Desert, 17, **57,**

57-61, **58, 59, 60, 61**
  India, 17, 39, 51
Australia, 9, 14, 17, 18,
    23, 33, 39

bacteria, 21, 56
bajadas, 23-24
basin deserts, 17, 54-57
birds, **31,** 33, 42, 47, **47,** 59,
    64-65, 69
buttes, 22, **23**

clouds, 10-11
coastal deserts, 39, **62,** 63-69
conservation, 72-73

desertification, 71
desert pavement, 21
dune fields, 52
dunes, 10, **16,** 18-19, **19,**
    40-41, 58, 65
dust storms, 41

ecosystems, 25, **69,** 69-73
  See also food chain
erosion, 56
Eurasia, 51, 52

farming, 15, 19, 44, 55-57,
    71, **71**
fires, 57

floods, 6-7, 13-15
fog, 63, 64-65, 68
food chain, 8, 25, **30,** 31, **31,**
    32, 33, 36, 42, 55-56,
    64-65, 69
frost, 41, 45
fungi, 21, 25, 56

gravel plains, 66-67

habitats, 9, 11, 44, 73
Hadley cell, 10
hamadas, 21
high-pressure systems,
    10-11
hot deserts, 9-10, **11,** 18, 35,
    39-49, **40,** 52
humans, 15, 19, 21, 37, **37,**
    41, 43-44, 55-57, 61, **61,**
    69, 69-73

insects, 15, 25, 28, **35,** 35-36,
    45, **64,** 65, 69
irrigation, 71

Madagascar, 63
Mideast
  Arabian peninsula, 17-
    18, 21-22, 39, 42, **42,**
    70, **71**
  Iran, 20-21, 51

Negev (Israel), 40
   winds, 41
minerals, **16,** 21, 69, **69,** 70,
   72
mountains, 12, 17, 22, 41, 49,
   54, 54-55, 58, **62,** 67

nights, 7, 11, **11,** 35
nomads, 44, 55, 61, **61**
North America, **8,** 14, 29,
   29, 41, 48
   Baja California, 63
   Big Bend, **52**
   Chihuahuan Desert, 39,
     49
   Death Valley, 45
   Grand Staircase-
     Escalante, **24**
   Great Basin Desert, 17,
     54-57, 70, 72, **72**
   Mojave Desert, 39, **45,**
     45-46, 48
   Salt Flats, 20, **20**
   Sonoran Desert, **11, 38,**
     39, **46,** 46-47, **47,** 72-73,
     73
nuclear weapons, 72, **72**

oases, 58, 61
oceans, 11-12, 46, 51, 63

currents, 64, 67-68
oil, 70

patina, 21
piedmont, 23-24
plants, 6, **8, 13,** 14-15, 22, 24,
   29, 38, 45, 45-47, **46, 47,**
   49, 52-53, 56-57, **62,**
   66-67, **67**
   adaptations, 28-31, **30**
   algae, 56
   epiphytic, 68-69
   mosses/lichens, 22, 56,
     66
   See also bacteria
plateaus, 21, 52, 58
protozoa, 27-28

rain, 6-7, 10, 13-14, 28, 31,
   49, 51, 63, 65
range deserts, 17
rivers, 6-7, 14-15, **15,** 21-22,
   27, 55, 65-66, 69
rocks, 21-22, **24**

salinization, 71
salt flats, **20,** 20-21, 52
salt pans, 25
sand fields, 17-18, 52
sand storms, 58

seasons, 10, 13, **38,** 41, 45,
   49, 51, 63, 65, 68
shield-platform deserts, 17,
   21
snow, 45, 49, 51, **52, 54**
soil, 10, 14, 17, 21, 23-24, 25,
   40, 52, 56
solar power, 44
South America
   Atacama Desert, 39, **62,**
     67-69, **68, 69,** 72
   Patagonian Desert, 12,
     50, 52-53

temperate deserts, 10, 13, 35,
   51-61, **53**
temperatures, 39-40, 49, 58,
   63

trees, 6, **8, 45,** 46-47, 57

volcanoes, 41

water
   aquifers, 15, 70, **71**
   standing, **26,** 27-28
   See also rain
weather systems, 10-11, 46
winds, 6, 12, 18-19, 25,
   40-41, 63, 69

Tom Warhol is a photographer, writer, and naturalist from Massachusetts, where he lives with his wife, their dog, and two cats. Tom holds both a BFA in photography and an MS in forest ecology. Tom has worked for conservation groups such as The Nature Conservancy, managing nature preserves, and The American Chestnut Foundation, helping to grow blight-resistant American chestnut trees. He currently works for the Massachusetts Riverways Program, helping to protect and restore rivers. He has also volunteered for the Vermont Raptor Center, caring for sick, injured, and resident hawks, eagles, and owls. In addition to the Earth's Biomes series, Tom has authored books for Marshall Cavendish Benchmark's AnimalWays series, including *Hawks* and *Eagles*. He also writes for newspapers such as the *Boston Globe*. His landscape, nature, and wildlife photographs can be seen in exhibitions, in publications, and on his Web site, www.tomwarhol.com.